Meliorism

Kenn Ho

Presentation by *BookLeaf Publishing*

Web: www.bookleafpub.com

E-mail: info@bookleafpub.com

ISBN: 9789395756457

First edition 2022

DEDICATION

ALL OF MY FANS AROUND THE WORLD.

ACKNOWLEDGEMENT

I always knew that I wanted to be an author and write a book one day.
Upon reaching destination, I encountered many disastrous attempts of my whatever life. I participated in a writing challenge to test my skills, enhance craft, and try something new. I was required to compose a new original poem, every day, for a certain number of days, until the project was complete. This manuscript complied together was the final product of the tedious task. Thus, my first ever, published poetry book. Thank you all for letting me live my dreams! I would like to acknowledge everyone involved in the metamorphosis of my brand. In no particular order, thank you to all of my loving and supporting family, friends, colleagues, mentors, peers, co-workers, collaborators, members of congregation, staff, union brothers, the haters who've motivated me to succeed, and anyone unmentioned by accident.
I would like to especially thank my "sister" Michelle for connecting me to Bruce Bang & iMix, Gloria Benedict at the Neal Hamil Agency, and The Spikes Management Company. My great pal and personal stylist, Cierra. Thank you, Vernessa and crew! Lastly, a special

shoutout to my buddy, Sylvia and her company Holistic Journey TLA for always being there for me, early morning and late nights, capturing these marvelous moments to share my experience with the world. I cannot express my gratitude. Teamwork made the dream work.

With Love,
Kenn

In Loving Memory
Tuan Hua Yang
(September 12, 1937 - November 14, 2021).

PREFACE

"Waiting for my time, feels like it's been my whole life now. Patience in my mind. I know, it will happen this lifetime."

Kenn Ho, born Kenny Ho Jr. (April 19,1991) is an American model, singer, songwriter, and actor. Originally from Texas, moved to Louisiana for a number of years and then moved back to Texas to assist in industry plans. After being a childhood model for JCPenney's (2006 Teen Choice Awards), Kenn Ho was destined to find his place as a star. After high school Kenn Ho traveled, meeting people and learning more about himself from the greatest teacher ever: life. Kenn Ho was able to meet people in the music industry with his amazing personality and charming looks and (maybe) luck. Kenn Ho has one album, one EP and one Christmas album. He recorded his first song Star in 2018, his song Ride (2019) has been his most streamed which was born out of a chaotic and hardworking past. Today Kenn Ho's latest and greatest single Me (2021) excites his fans for upcoming music.

Obeisance

Welcome to my book!
It is off the hook,
The fact you've taken a look.

Please, continue on.

This is the interpretation of gold.
That is told subliminally in bold.
Explicitly, content in context.

I am excited that readers will see.
The other side of me.
I hope y'all enjoy reading, my poetry!

(DIY) - Do It Yourself -

Let's begin at the root of the problem.
Authenticate and handle matters as necessary.
The approach is unknown and random.

Result may vary depending on action.
Reach for all the customization possible.
Create a version and visualize accordingly.
Starts with erasing negativity.

All Of The Above.

It really is, badly!
How, you are, sadly!
Around, the molecules.

Depth of science, beyond idiomatic.
Constant lacking and slacking of the irregular.

Begin the new chapter of living.
Loosen up energy and travel the world.
I know you don't care, silly.

Yucky!!

The definition of zero.
Loud, and draw attention.
What a drag it is to deal with.

Shame as usual.
As, very never, by any means.
That, to fill, up space.

You, are in, for it.
Non, every and all uselessness 24/7.
Urban.

(release)

Yup.
You, forgot, something.
Right?
You, make me giggle.
Okay.

Bop that boom-bah class again honey.
Glam, and strutting a skip.
Perfection from the non-existent string tied
holding together imagination.

Do collect yourself and relax.
Cache, tract, whirlwind-whack.
With purpose empty as confusion valid.

(Take a breath)
Exclamation point!

Inclement

Nothing to do.
It's absolutely boring.
There is a solution.

Attempt to focus and alert senses.
Participation is a factor.
Notice the measure of procrastination.
Obligation is required for survival.

Hydration is the basics.
Staying active is a goal.
Consistent stimulation of productivity.

Destruction

Yawning, as the luminescence beams.
Cold, wearing high seams.
Sun, performing calendar analog.
Shut the luck, grunt.
Your ship has sunk, slam dunk!

Lobby and observe.
Locate answer and execute a solution.
Having technical difficulty?

A peripheral mess up.
Please, forgive me!
I can not force you to do anything you don't
want to.

abracadabra*

Turned between destinies.
North, South, East, and West.
Such comprehensive camouflage.

Compete relationship gone stale,
Lying being the main source.
Genius master of a folding artist.

Oh, so simple and darling.
Frequency quality everyone fancy.
Magic crossed forever and ever.
Over and out.

Delinquency

Lost communication fashion.
Rectify passion constantly.
One hundred percent.

Type of co-exist sight,
At the might and height.
Zigzag and fly a kite!
While we take a hike and like.

Whew Chile, come and vibe crescendo fallen
star babe, casa grandeur kind of loophole.

Always try,
Halt, thee most haughty version of self.
Disco ball is optional for the partying.
Standard pieces of a puzzle.
Guess doubt and be at your highest, shimmering
all the time.

Sincerely,

Beware from the abandoned.
Pain from exposure is too surreal.
Detach and process positivity.

It requires much in me,
To acknowledge facts, you are so, really!
Heal the wounds within.

Good morning friend, how are you?
Complementary rambunctious conversation.

The End.

It's too hard to change.
Really, can't complain.
Stay, in your lane.
Or you won't be the same!

Don't be accountable for failure.

Faith and trust for a happily ever after.
Fairy tale kiss frogs a fairy godmother.
Earth night smoke and reflective mirrors.

Once upon a time, in a land far away.

Avoid the disarray.
Membrane instantly insane.
Thank you for your patience.

♥

Be blessed things happened, the way it did.

Rejoice with devotion.
Decoration in disguise.
Promises to deadline a decline.

Out of line aptitude conservations.
Corrupted attitude conversations.

Push thy aggression towards progression.

Indecisive pettiness um, ratification.

Declaration masterpiece exclusive planet articles
of incorporation.

Don't rally and let the brain develop.

You got this.

Redundancy

You love confrontation.

I worked hard for this moment.

Shenanigans are deep inside me.

Rigor persuasion ignore without the inevitable, a real deal plot presumed.

Assuming that you are going to be leaving me here, by myself, to clean up your mess.

Yeah, right!

Better think again.

In fact, you should be prepared to pay repercussions.

Won't be over until I end.

Speak up, louder for entertainment.

hi9H

The drama escalates,
Resulting at a exponential rate.

Mega crystal shadow traveling mojo.
Indescribable amount of classiness.
Splurging in the fast lane.

Blow eskimo kisses honey angel pooh!
Holla, holler.
Too damn close!
So, fucking hilarious.

It is a joke to make effects last longer.

The spell is wearing off,
I am now deteriorating.

Where is the money?
Laughing out loud!
Write about money.

Adherence Infraction

Are you ever into expensive taste?
Fluctuations in the universe.
You're so multi-talented!

Violation without warning is scattered and
soothing.
Functioning is the pretty alibi.
Extremely much important, especially not the
same.

Shambles is a definite degree
but doesn't sum up completely.

Too much risky manipulation.

Gone missing, lost, or stolen.
Per compromise, adjourned differences.
Hear carefully, it could occur.

A plan can fall apart and highly sensitive
material waste.

Silence is a transaction for a scavenger building
a travesty.

Ultimately, being born to this devastation is the way.

Peace out!

:-)

I love you.
That is the memo.
I'm right here.
Temperature of restlessness.

English punctuation is fragmented grammar.
The verbal is most likely incorrect.
Precision conquered and the product is now
prompt.

So, I can't make believe and play pretend.

The weather outside the sarcasm.

Rebellion on a whim.

National daydream gone bad.

Like, simplicity salvation.

Method trending all eternity.

Twirl

Winning is delicious.

Beauty is nice.

Thought it was hip, doing that skip, whilst
pouting my lips.

Counting the rifts from so many slips existing.

Isn't it dope with no hope, and you cannot cope.

Get a grip and sip on something yummy.

CoNcOcTiOn

I have regret not expressed.
I have made a way to re-invest.
I hate feeling compressed.

Dress, as I begin a new quest.
I confess, I am no longer suppressed.
I suggest, it has to be addressed.

Requiring request for zest, thine can digest.

INTERLUDE

The trauma lasts, and my head is pounding.
The afflictions wound substantially.
Inaccuracy and an ego.

No one knows what happened.

How, did I get here?
I'm so tired.
You can see it, in my face, a poor alternative.

I can't change my actions.
Nothing can replace the time spent.

Lost youth,
Past or present?
I go on wondering, as there is no future.

Aromatic air my breeches,
The same street and wall.
Everything, I see and touch.
This isn't the life for me anymore.

I'm alone now.

What's done is done.

What is my purpose?
I look so happy.
Loneliness.

I feel like a slave.
I can't escape and cope.
Please, dis-connect, reset, and turn off.

Repeat Offender

It's that time of the day, again.
I'm off, to an early start.
Not by choice, and it's pre-determined.

Years have turned into decades.
I'm constantly reminded.

I'm quiet, and quite sure, nothing is going to
change.
I want to quit.

Coded gibberish meant for debate, extension
from daily retort.

Understood as pellucid.
The coordinate is incorrect, a total mathematical
error loss.

Smiling mesh rhetorical, changes perception as
always.

Maybe a prayer will help.

∞

Sketch is a pure understatement.
Circling oscillation, and it continues - infinity.

I try avoiding, as if it will help.
I am aware but, so irritated.

It's the fact of the matter.

Sure, looks and sounds like me.
Plus, who are you going to believe?

The balance growing and maturing.
Are you ready?
I'm in the direct peak of calculation.

Let's go.
Some senseless increasing score,
Minus, two sides of a story.
Impeding impulse creates a new game.

One by one, combining with each other.

Backward and sideways, up and forth,
Never-ending, a google.